MAX BRETT
THE CONSEQUENCES

Ness Books

Contents

A Primer for the Reader to Understand
the Material in this Collection 7
On Being Right 15
      Interlude 16
They Are Gone 17
Responding to Crises 20
Jenner Againer 22
Dinner 23
      Interlude 25
Max Brett at the Association of Writers and
Writing Programs Conference and Bookfair
in Portland, Oregon 26
Suds 27
The Monster at the End of this Book 28
      Interlude 29
Mladen Stilinović, galerie frank elbaz 30
Paris/Parris/Le Maryland/Maryland 32
Fruit Baskets and Performance Evaluation 35
Jo 37
His 41
Hers 42
Hers (Continued) 43
Aspirational Daydreams Regarding the Reading
List of Susan Howe 44
Library Cormorant 45
Cardinals and Forced Marriages 46
Jordan 48

A Gift	51
MFS	54
HRBP	56
Qatar Airways Meal Optionality	57
Corgi!	58
Winter Pre-dawn Under Museum Lights	59
Angers (a Description of the Tapestries in the Hometown of the Proprietress of a Now-defunct Bean Store on rue Notre-Dame de Nazareth)	61
Why Time Passes Quickly	63
The State of Things	65
The Worship of Georges Perec	66
Musette: A Visit Thwarted	69
Interlude	72
The Making of the Nightly News	73
Friendship	75
La campagne	76
Glenstone	77
Ad Man Studies	79

A Primer for the Reader to Understand the Material in this Collection

Prior to the publication of *Nor Do These* in March 2019, my partner (the bipolar third party referenced in that book, hereafter referred to as "my partner," "the partner," "the bipolar third party," and "the third party") and their Norwegian forest cat left New York for Paris. (See *Nor Do These*.) The partner required a shift from New York noise, the festering trash piled on its corners and its visual specificities—a *fraîche* start. I remained in New York.

My inflexibilities, groundless suspicions and weakness produced a year with the third party that was sandpapery in its unpleasant friction. The Colombian composer and musician with whom the third party and I collaborated on an exquisite corpse exercise that spurred *Nor Do These* remained threatening: dynamic, grant-laden, ascendant, a beautiful *águila* in flight, Andean sun shining behind powerful and somehow transparent wings.

I was a minted poet-think tank professional in New York and I was alone.

A very brief period of intense relief and joyous solitude was followed by inertia-pain and persistent, alarming stomach pain that demanded a gastroenterologist.

I felt the thrum of abandonment. This called to mind earlier twinning, staggered abandonments that steer my unexamined life.

Those earlier abandonments led me to develop an expertly weighted and beautifully pigeon feather-green coat of supercilious armor that I wore all the time and that deflected everything. It was expertly crafted by a community in the 17th century that numbered 10,000 artisans. Today, only six such craftspeople remain, with four apprentices.

Despite expertly crafted hinges worth more than the diamonds embedded in the coat, this armor was stripped off me in a brusque, nonsexual, nonconsensual armor-removal, as a gust of unexpected wind would carry off an Alençon lace bridal veil, labored over by 100 lace-makers for an entire year. I was naked and submerged in green. A narrow brown cloud of destabilization cut through the green, spewing from a faulty destabilization-spigot fed by a massive deep-sea deposit of destabilization presided over by an Anglophone CEO focused on destabilization efficiencies and maximizing shareholder value. (The CEO would deflect responsibility for the malfunction of the spigot in a series of interviews that infuriated newsrooms, that infuriated and depressed viewers around the world, reminded as they were that governments answer to corporations. The CEO wondered on the record when their life would return to normal.) A static camera continuously filmed ghostly images of the disaster.

The bipolar third party's constricting and guiding wires had bent me into a formidable (yet diminutive and constrained) prize bonsai on a shelf of bonsais cared for by an Illinois Montessori school teacher. Consider the influence of the third party. How much of my work could I even be said to be responsible for? I pondered this amid piles of clothes, dishes, bottles and Queens Public Library books alone in New York, destabilized.

I thought about "starting over."

My aim would be to process abandonment, to start over, to grow. This would require focus and work, objects of disinclination. My focus, wandering, was drawn to *the* distracting figure, the figure of advertising professional Mike Immerman, who existed thousands of miles away. I would focus on Mike for some time, longer than necessary.

I then thought of Peter Lacy and Francis Bacon. I thought of Lacy idolizing Fats Waller and Bacon idolizing Lacy's calves and the both of them fighting and thriving through instability, driven by instability, feeding on instability. I thought about Lacy being sexually dominant in his relationship with Bacon and simultaneously emotionally controlled by Bacon. The calves, pulsating, butternut calves. The quiet command of those calves. After Lacy told Bacon he should consider himself (Lacy) "as dead," Lacy fled, Bacon lost it, and a year later, Lacy would invite Bacon to Tangier to begin again. In *Happy Together*, Ho Po-Wing has the same proposal to Lai Yiu-Fai as Lacy did to Bacon:

"Let's start over."

This collection came about as I processed my relationship to abandonment and my fear of being abandoned, wrestled and reckoned with the towering sexual iconography of Mike Immerman, examined submission to a higher order of being or dominant other (in the terrestrial sphere), contemplated the source of the things I enjoy and the suffering it brings those who labor on those loved things, and developed invented narratives around Paris. I shifted the routine of running up and down stairs in Doughboy Park, sometimes with Alicia and sometimes with Victoria, to stairs on the Canal Saint-Martin, watching cormorants shake their wings dry in front of indigent refugees, indigent EU passport holders and all manner of privileged people.

The Norwegian forest cat died of cancer. The bipolar third party partner lived, expanding, consuming, becoming, becoming, driving and circling better self-awareness.

I was not abandoned. I had been abandoned.

I tell myself this on the stairs, watching a swan chase ducklings, very threateningly, upsetting children walking with guardians.

This is a collection of transitory and permanent attachments.

The Consequences

On Being Right

My partner says my eyes are blue.

But I know that they are green.

"I am leaving you forever," my partner says.

*

Denial, avoidance, solitude and longing were the touchstones of a meditative period of wheel-spinning and self-pleasuring alone in terrific quiet.

*

They Are Gone

"Thought regains its place in poop."

I woke up very early in the mornings and watched Jean-Luc Godard films during this period. I would think of how quiet it was.

This was in the two-bedroom apartment in Sunnyside I had shared with the partner.

I had experienced intense gastrointestinal distress for several weeks and consulted a handsome gastroenterologist, who ordered a scan, but seemed convinced this was anxiety. He advised me that I was experiencing "asymmetrical stress warfare waged by a third party state actor, metaphorically."

A fly bounced against his office window, moving toward the light.

I had once gifted a cassette tape of *The Little Mermaid* original soundtrack to my partner just over there in the dark where the couch used to be in the Sunnyside apartment. (The couch had been donated in the lead up to the move to Paris along with most of our furniture.) But we didn't have a cassette deck. My partner called it "a most violent gesture."

This two-bedroom apartment was rented from John, a chain-smoking Greek, and his son, Kosta, who resembled in physical and emotional aspect a Haribo jelly bean, with almost vanishing features and a gently curved, tubular, unnaturally colored body. Kosta was now a father himself. Kosta was born in this apartment, not far from where I was sitting, in one of the few remaining chairs in the space, watching Godard.

Decades ago, John, smoking, and all of the neighbors watched on, cheering as fluids poured through the living room and his wife gave birth to Kosta, just over there, where the birthing stain resembled Switzerland. Decades later, this birth spot was where the Norwegian forest cat used to flop over and stare fixedly at the ceiling, legs splayed, watching the ghosts that watched Kosta grow up with his mother and father in Sunnyside.

Cats love birth flow-stained parquet.

Kosta attended Aviation High School and was one of the strongest airplane engine repair persons at LaGuardia. His favorite airplane engines were Rolls-Royce aircraft engines, which "push the boundaries of what is possible" and are part of the Trent family of "aeroplane" engines.

Kosta's high-flying airplane engine repair person career was grounded (his wings were clipped) when his father required his assistance in the family business—maintaining a series of properties in Queens he purchased after arriving from somewhere in Greece. Kosta's colleagues at LaGuardia threw him a big party with an airplane engine-shaped cake when he left to help his father.

Kosta was there with me as I prepared to leave. Kosta told me that change was positive and that leaving New York was exciting and new and growth-oriented, and, should I ever want to return, that he and John would likely have a rental unit waiting for me. Kosta said all this softly, kindly, like a jelly bean, wary of the wreck before him, but essentially radiating compassion.

Responding to Crises

You might wonder during your evening constitutional or your morning walk in the bright sunlight through a crowded urban area about the appeal of soft targets and crowded urban areas to active shooters who aim to capitalize on the "inherent openness" of crowded areas and soft targets.

The United States Cybersecurity and Infrastructure Security Agency (CISA) has considered the dilemma you face as a person in the United States of America and elsewhere.

And it is natural to feel anxiety with regard to situations that you cannot control.

While mass shootings and gun violence feel more and more a shared and understood experience in the United States, perhaps you have not considered the risk to your person that a Vehicle Ramming Attack poses, in the United States and elsewhere.

Bollards, heavy planters and barricades are useful for creating standoff distances between people and a Vehicle Ramming Attack. Such structures must be sufficiently anchored and proportioned to withstand the force of a Vehicle Ramming Attack. In a situation without such protective measures, one would do best to run away from the Vehicle doing the Ramming with all possible haste.

The Battery Park Vehicle Ramming Attack took place on a path for bikers and runners.

Red flags for vehicle rental industry workers who evaluate customers as potential perpetrators of a Vehicle Ramming Attack: customers who insist on cash payment to rent a vehicle and visible signs of nervousness referred to by the U.S. Department of Homeland Security as "the Vehicle Ramming Attack twitch."

Again, run hard if a Vehicle Ramming Attack appears to be in progress.

We could all do with more "inherent openness" with regard to the possibility of experiencing a Vehicle Ramming Attack.

Soft targets and crowded places include, but are not limited to, "schools, sports venues, transportation systems or hubs, shopping venues, bars and restaurants, hotels, places of worship, tourist attractions, theaters and civic spaces."

La duquesa es:
Esposa
Mujer
Marida
Alma
Musa
Ardilla ambiciosa

Dinner

As he assembled a bowl of turmeric-ginger-garlic lentils, quinoa, avocado and yogurt (yoghurt), he thought about the quantity or volume of water necessary to grow lentils and the deforestation in Michoacán from avocado farming and the Avocado Bosses of Michoacán and the drug gangs and drug cartels siphoning taxes from these avocado farmers and avocado farmers imposing martial law in their communities and vigilante avocado farmer gangs in open-bed trucks with guns and a notice in his regularly visited grocery store above an empty display normally reserved for a pyramid of avocados explaining that avocados cost three dollars apiece that day because of a strike by farmers in Mexico (in Michoacán, though the text didn't specify the state) and he thought of the Chobani yogurt (yoghurt) in his dinner and the Chobani facility in Twin Falls, Idaho, where the third party, the partner, was born, and the combined methane flatulence of the cows and the canyon of black volcanic rock in Twin and the orange Maine coon cat in Twin named Cheddar and the proud dairy people of Twin and the off-white Church of Latter Day Saints temple in Twin and the beneficence of Chobani CEO Hamdi Ulukaya in Twin and Hamdi's work on behalf of refugees, and how, if he wanted to, Hamdi could act as a sort of Untouchable Yogurt (yoghurt) Caudillo (UYC) there in Twin and of course then he thought of longtime Idaho Governor Butch Otter and then he thought of quinoa, grown in

Bolivia and Peru, and the necessity of maintaining fragile quinoa diversity despite despite *despite* demand for a narrow variety of quinoa, causing farmers to abandon outlier grains, farmers who would need to be compensated monetarily to maintain those grains, who in the future might face quinoa grower competition from China, India and Nepal.

*

Rather than constructively processing my relationship with the bipolar third party—the partner—their childhood in Idaho, their life in New York and its place in my life, their new life in Paris and my loss and loneliness, I turned my attention to my impending, massive, overwhelming, character-changing literary success in the bloody, scatological, moist, earthy arena of avant-garde poetry with Nor Do These. *I contemplated my public celebration and also "fleshy delight" in the form and shape of an opponent and verbal combatant—a friend I despise —Mike Immerman. I began to be obsessed with the idea of him replacing me at upcoming literary conferences, acting as my stand-in. Those who assured me they understood the arena were very clear that "physically beautiful poets are the only ones who make it" as they bit into large apples and stared through me. It made sense. It all made sense.*

*

Max Brett at the Association of Writers and Writing Programs Conference and Bookfair in Portland, Oregon

Max Brett deputized his friend Mike Immerman to attend the Association of Writers and Writing Programs Conference and Bookfair in Portland, Oregon, as him, Max Brett. A post-conference media profile of Mike Immerman as Max Brett began like this:

"Max Brett, with squinty eyes and chestnut curls, rode into #AWP19 on a speedometer-less Honda motorcycle as an unknown. He left an impression: a free-associating brain addled by attention deficit disorder behind Semitic good looks attached to a simian frame with seemingly limitless sexual endurance, with a propensity to touch and taste everything he came into contact with. He lives a life of magnetism. He lacks shame and self-consciousness. He is liberated. Max Brett stalked the conference halls, inviting fellow conference-goers to sniff his middle and index finders, smiling broadly, telling them, 'You tell *me* whether everything is OK.'"

"Why do I sexualize Mike in this way?" I thought.

Mike is a person with thoughts and feelings. Mike is more than a raw conduit of sexual vitality.

I then visualized Mike taking a bird bath in a stainless steel sink in a Los Angeles Public Library bathroom.

Suds

Strategically placed soap suds obscure and tantalizingly hint at the nudity of a smiling, squinting young ad man and filmmaker and editor named Mike Immerman. Mike has emerged from a circular tub full of roiling perfumed water in a redwood cabin in Big Sur surrounded by luminous candles that he shares, tonight, with his partner, who works for a Los Angeles cultural institution or a zoo or a newspaper, and who is responsible for the photo. The partner of Mike is pregnant with their first child. Neither of them know this. The photo was appropriated by a Los Angeles artist. Enhanced and replicated, versions of the photo surrounded visitors to the Los Angeles gallery where *Ad Man Studies (After On Kawara)* went up years later. The work now lives in a large beige private residence designed by Tadao Ando in Ketchum, Idaho, where, this evening, Chobani CEO Hamdi Ulukaya soaked in them, for the millionth time, and tugged at lubricated tendrils of potential meaning.

The Monster at the End of this Book

I have broken my earlier commitment to refrain from sexualizing Mike Immerman and I commit for the duration of the rest of this, however long it ends up being, not to do this thing where I rob Mike of his identity and personhood and make him a nonverbal fuckslut.

The transition to Paris was not without its small and large kerfuffles and squabblings, misunderstandi-doodles and mad, insane battles of will between myself and the third party, the partner. We entered into our long fencing matches, wearing our white costumes, but maskless (for a time), nerves antingle (vibrating), with a will to dominate, to degrade, to humiliate, to drink the blood of, but never to truly wound each other. This was about learning how the métro worked, what baguettes really were and what we would do, especially what we would do for Eurobucks, different from Freedombucks in size, color, and other respects, but used in exchange for goods, just like Freedombucks are in the U.S.A. Adventures in libraries and bookstores, solitary vacant observation and fumbling contemplation ensued. I thought about Georges Perec and how much of life in Paris might be staring at inanimate and animate things for extended periods of time, without purpose. We were starting again. Starting over. Starting over. Now.

Mladen Stilinović, galerie frank elbaz

I last saw the work of Mladen Stilinović in Ciudad Universitaria in Mexico City after riding a Metrobus south forever and walking through penetrating sunlight to MUAC, which had a career retrospective.

The piece in Mexico City that stuck in my brain was video of a frog launching itself from position to position and Mladen's Croatian voice repeating:

"Great show."
"Great show."
"Great show."

to each jump.

And now I am in Paris and I am seeing Mladen's work at galerie frank elbaz and a fire alarm is registering its low energy level with periodic chirps and there is nothing I can do to steer the situation.

It is not in my control.

Mladen has pasted a black and white photo of a television to a white sheet of paper and the TV is saying (in a "talk" bubble):

"kukurika."

"kukurika."

And I am sweating as I write with a blue ballpoint and the paper is resistant to being written upon.

Mladen documents himself photographically and he looks very skinny and delicate and effeminate and he smokes a cigarette and records the holes in his shoes.

Paris/Parris/Le Maryland/Maryland

There are several tabac-bars called Le Maryland in Paris and there is one in the third arrondissement that is enjoyable.

Le Maryland has warm yellow lights that illuminate menus and notebooks and set off the red ink from a Pentel Energel Liquid Gel Ink pen made in Japan, arguably the best pen for writing, the light producing a really pleasing combination of red and yellow.

And the server who sings to himself as he serves knows the mannerisms of customers after a single visit because he is an expert observer of his clientele and their needs and their little tics.

So he knows one customer can't get enough olives and he knows when the last pit will hit the tray and he'll bring out another tray and it would probably go on all night if the client or the server wanted to test resolve on either end and the spicy little olives are covered in oregano and a red wine goes nice with these tiny free olives and stress is peeling off walled in by beige canyons underneath yellow lights while writing with red ink and the question arises and lingers (though it is not pressing) why they (the proprietors) named this bar, this tabac, Le Maryland.

Poor immigrants from the Eastern Shore or Olney or Wheaton or Baltimore County or Baltimore or St. Mary's or Gaithersburg or Bethesda or Wheaton or Annapolis or Potomac or Silver Spring (you understand) left the fallow or arid or fertile or barren, maybe barren, soil of Maryland, their home attacked by big blue crabs, with the cruel caudillo Parris Glendening (not yet governor of the state of Maryland) exacting tribute and the patriarch or matriarch of this little family telling future Governor Parris Glendening, or pleading:

"Parris, the crabs are pinching! As our lord, you are bound to protect us from the ceaseless pinching of these blue, blue crabs!"

And Parris, brushing the dust off his leopard coat and eating a seared slab of foie gras sandwiched between two lemon zest macarons, languidly suggesting that the serf family unlucky enough to be born on his vast Maryland holdings set out cans of Old Bay Seasoning to signal a warning to the crabs—malicious Parris—and the family realizing that they had to leave their home and move to Paris.

And they had to run a tabac. They would sell tobacco and alcohol to strangers.

It would be everything their Maryland, their nightmare, wasn't.

The olives would be bountiful.

Olive-abundance would be the byword/s at Le Maryland.

And we will never speak of the place we left, the little family's members told one another, but the blazing neon cursive of the Le Maryland sign will beguile our Parisian neighbors.

We'll never forget what Parris did to us.

We'll never forget what Paris did for us.

Fruit Baskets and Performance Evaluation

Thank you for the variety of plums on offer.

It wasn't made clear during onboarding here in the nondescript suburbs of Paris near the île de la Grande Jatte that every Monday employees would have access to giant wicker baskets full of plums.

Purple and green and tiny orange-yellow plums that are called Mirabelle plums.

Reine-Claude plums.

They are so cold and sweet.

There is a crispness and a softness.

A crisp-soft interplay.

The performance review was negative, alarming and anxiety inducing, a diuretic. Concerns about the culture fit were expressed. Drinking coffee all morning and eating all of these plums has produced a powerful laxative effect.

And now, the pressing need, the imperative, is to clean excrement off a 2014-2015 Mexico home jersey with its lightning bolts of white and red almost conveying the force and not at all conveying the randomness, the chaos, of the shitting all over clothes in an office restroom, alone and sweating.

Still, the plums were really very good.

Cold and firm and sometimes sweet and sometimes tart. Everything you want in a plum.

There was a sense on the métro that shit-covered workers must ride home every day in this way, hiding the shame of performance reviews and of plums.

Jo

"In the Marais, there are Jews," Jo says during our lunch. There is a slight smile from Jo. "This is unique in Paris."

This statement seems inaccurate. I am certain that it is inaccurate. I remain engaged, green-eyed.

"They are wearing the jackets and the hats and they have their—I don't know how you say it—their *curls*?"

Jo smiles once more. I wonder where this is going. I maintain eye contact.

Jo continues: "When I was in New York living on West 34th Street in…" and then she describes a sort of dormitory facility with many apartments and without a religious affiliation. Jo makes it clear that such a facility in France would almost always have a religious affiliation, but this one where Jo lived was started by an heir of the Macy's fortune. Jo corrected herself here: "a protégé or protégés of an heir to the Macy's fortune."

They are the Webster brothers, Charles and Josiah, who aimed to provide a residence where unmarried women could live affordably regardless of their religious affiliation or nationality. The Webster brothers seem to have understood that upon arriving in New York, the women who worked at Macy's were set upon by male menace and all manner of exploitation and discrimination. The brothers decided that their fortune, made off the labor of these women, should at least in part help to support their welfare.

This facility, the Webster House, now primarily houses students and interns for international organizations like the United Nations in Turtle Bay. The architect of the U.N. building is Charles-Édouard Jeanneret, who renamed himself Le Corbusier. Le Corbusier believed any person could reinvent themselves.

In one United Nations sublevel (for the building extends underground) Jo visited during her time in New York, interning scientists studied water samples and mosquito larvae in an effort to control and perhaps even eradicate Zika, the objectively terrifying mosquito-borne deformer of infants.

Complicator of pregnancies.

Male carriers of the virus sometimes have no symptoms and can pass the virus to women, as well as pregnant women.

Has Zika been eradicated? This thought is not easily driven away.

Jo describes "the phenomenon of seeing so many Orthodox Jews in New York" as being "*most* exciting."

"Communities of Orthodox Jews don't exist in Paris," she says, "not of that size, not with... their *little curls*," she emphasizes, smiling still, "and their *hats*."

Paris features plaques on the walls of current and former schools that explain that students were sent to death camps.

Jo is Catholic and in her twenties. Jo emphasizes that she is Catholic.

Catholic bishops in France initially endorsed the Vichy government and its legal decrees excluding Jews from public life. The bishops "publicly venerated the new [Vichy] regime and encouraged the laity to follow in its footsteps," according to the scholarship of Aliza Luft, assistant professor of sociology at UCLA. In 1942, the bishops reversed course—the clergy and the laity mobilized to help to save the Jews of France. Deportation rates fell. Luft's book, *Sacred Treason* (currently under contract, publication date unknown), aims to show how "public defections by prominent authorities can shape how genocides unfold." The book probes the linkage of moral judgments and moral actions—essentially, when we can expect people to act on their moral beliefs.

I think for an instant of being fed splintery Christ-body wafers—as many as I want—by Jo as heavy clouds of incense spurt from a thurible Jo swings rapidly, sensually, with a lot of eye contact. We are atop an orange marble altar draped in vine-green silk covered in yellowish candles and beige wax drips continuously onto the fabric around us.

And then the lunch hour with Jo concludes.

His

For him:

Sultaines-brand chickpeas in their juices.

The brand features a baby tooth-white Moorish fortress with a massive turret, its rounded walls all bleached white by searing sun somewhere in MENA or perhaps Spain.

Four camels are in the foreground and a single palm tree is in front of them.

The scene is devoid of people, or people have fled the scene. Perhaps their essence remains, their spirit, but they are not there. Or maybe they are outside the frame.

Maybe the camels have taken over. Camel-plots and camel-intrigue. The sum of all fears: A beast of burden reaches sentience and overthrows your system of governance.

Hers

For her:

Haribo Goldbears.

Haribo was started in Bonn.

These gummies are for children and adults.

Since 1922, Haribo has understood that determining a specific age group in its product marketing would be a limiting factor in gummy consumption.

Their greens, yellows and reds are not the result of artificial coloring.

Hers (Continued)

A documentary produced in 2017 depicted the horrible working conditions faced by Brazilians in Piauí, Ceará, Maranhão, Bahia and Rio Grande do Norte as workers harvested the carnauba wax necessary to make gummy bears shine. The documentary also noted Haribo action to disrupt the organizing efforts of striking carnauba wax plantation workers, who earn the equivalent of EUR 10 per day without access to toilets and without access to potable water.

Some of the contracted workers are allegedly children.

Haribo's gelatin supplier Gelita makes its gelatin from pigs in overcrowded pig farms. The pigs are submerged in their own shit. Gummies are made of the skin, bones and connective tissue of a vast community of allegedly abused German pigs.

Haribo has denied the allegations in the press report this is derived from.

Aspirational Daydreams Regarding the Reading List of Susan Howe

In times of isolation, pain and futility, I like to think Susan Howe is reading my work and enjoying a bottle of La Bastide Saint-Vincent Mademoiselle Garance, a fruity and spicy Syrah from Violès, "a commune in the Vaucluse department in the Provence-Alpes-Côte d'Azur region in southeastern France."

The wine store employee who sells me this bottle invariably describes it as "fresh," an adjective whose contours are malleable.

Fraîche.

Library Cormorant

A bipolar schizophrenic aunt spent entire days in Berkeley public libraries reading entire books in single sittings wearing dirty clothes and mumbling off and on for years and years and years before her sanity evaporated and she spent her hours alone, mumbling continuously, completely unaccountable to anyone in a self-imposed exile made comic by its proximity to relatives who would no longer willingly subject themselves to the pain and chaos she inflicted.

Cardinals and Forced Marriages
to Fiona, for Fiona

Blue dusk, pedestrians and two-note sirens in winter ring outside the Seine-facing windows of the once-private, now-public library of an Italian cardinal who made himself French.

His life was unbroken shrewd diplomacy for 17th century warlike France.

One of his major wins was an arranged marriage between María Theresa and Louis XIV, a golden affirmation of cousin-fucking and a bridge to peace between France and Spain.

Five of María's six children died in early childhood.

Louis had many other partners.

Scholars see María as Catholic-pious, virtuous: a hopeless milky cuckquean and lover of God isolated in a vast palace untouched and laughed at who died of an arm abscess at 44.

What did she do?

What did she read?

Who did she talk to?

María is forever understood as an instrument of peace mocked or pitied by contemporaries.

Her marriage helped secure the fortune of the cardinal who built the mustard-columned bust-ridden library, formerly just his, now open to readers for an annual fee.

María's bust is not here.

Jordan

I promised Jordan that I would write something about him.

But I made the promise knowing very little about him.

So I researched Jordan and the life he has orchestrated and decided to combine this very casual research with my brief tableside experience in which his interest in me was sharp and then faded and resurged and then faded and then was absolutely gone:

Jordan is happy and confident enough to shout out potential sexual partners on the street when visiting his hometown, Paris, from Milan, where he lives and works.

"You're the man for me!" he will say to a stranger.

Jordan loves horses and seems to have stable access somewhere in Italy.

He has a wispy beard.

His companion this evening has very smooth, very fine, very nearly hairless skin. Swiss accountant skin.

Having stopped the passerby in his tracks with his catcall, Jordan will offer to do a line of cocaine off the stranger's erect penis.

Jordan is interested in Godard, he says. He says he has not read any Toni Morrison, though he is wearing a shirt with the word "Milkman" on it, along with the framed face of a man with stubble, head tilted back, with a trickle of breast milk running down his chin. There is no accounting for the discrepancy.

I think of the scene in *Vivre sa vie* where the protagonist, a sex worker, is driven via car toward her death in the outskirts, I think, of Paris.

It's a beautiful sequence and ends.

A quiet and rambling and beautiful film with limited insight into the realities of sex work.

Then I think of Jordan at runway shows in Milan, loud and corporate, with Thomas, his strained, foxlike friend, breaking out of accountancy and into the realm of High Fashun and electronic music.

Jordan and Thomas on the streets of Paris smoking Marlboros (I think) and Jordan shouting at people, catcalling, fearless.

I think a lot about people who understand that nothing horrible will ever happen to them.

He really was very nice if somewhat single-minded and sexual harassment-forward.

And Jordan holding his own knees and sitting on a rock in Cala Rossa, Sicilian sailboats having a sailboat conference, everything serene and warm.

And the chalky cliffs of Scala dei Turchi, chalky as the cocaine bumped off an erect penis somewhere in Paris.

Not mine.

A Gift

Michelle de Simon told me I should read Philip Roth.

Michelle is 5 feet tall.

Michelle looks up at people and tells them what to do.

Michelle has given birth four times without epidurals.

Michelle said, "No doulas."

Michelle fought off a rabid elk with a burning branch.

Michelle mulches.

Michelle sutured a deep thigh wound with floss and a fishbone.

Michelle told the moon not to rise and it didn't.

Michelle climbed a tall tree and screamed at crows.

Michelle did her homesteading in Maine.

Michelle recommended Philip Roth to me.

"Toni Morrison is shit," she said. "You have to read Philip Roth."

And I said, "I didn't say anything about Toni Morrison."

Michelle smacked me in the mouth.

Michelle said, "Make eye contact when you are speaking with me."

When I got to be older, I realized that Michelle was not the ultimate arbiter of the merit of the literary production of Toni Morrison.

At the time, Michelle seemed to be exactly this—my experience was limited.

After 20 years I had shaken myself of her influence and, hands trembling, read the first novel Toni Morrison published.

I then read all the Toni Morrison that there was.

I went on to sell many copies of Toni Morrison novels and essays to customers at Shakespeare & Co during a one-week fixed-term contract.

The buyers would come in completely energized from the experience of touristic wanderings in Paris and were highly susceptible to my suggestions and recommendations.

As customers left with *Jazz* and *Paradise*, I was wary of the vengeful spirit of Michelle, a sort of copy of her, as she is very much alive, in or near San Antonio, but I imagined a spectral form of her, with the blondness of her, behind every bookshelf. Michelle can and has duplicated herself as needs arose. And arise.

I was sure that she would strike me down.

I still find myself looking for her behind shelves.

Two men sit down on the gray leather sofa of the Médiathèque Françoise Sagan, a great Paris library. One wears Weimaraner-gray, ankle-high suede boots. The other wears black-and-crocodile green reflective acrylic clown shoes with limp cadmium socks. They are signing and clicking animatedly with each other because they are hearing impaired.

The meeting is a sort of book club. The book they are communicating about is Tom Clancy's *Patriot Games*.

Tom Clancy is possibly the most famous and successful Marylander writer, with over 100 million copies sold.

He was born in Baltimore and died in Baltimore.

He owned part of the Baltimore Orioles for a time.

Patriot Games was his third novel. Though the forever protagonist Jack Ryan first appeared in *The Hunt for Red October*, *Patriot Games* takes place before the events of that novel and is, chronologically, Ryan's first appearance.

Jack Ryan Jack Ryan Jack Ryan.

In *Patriot Games*, Jack Ryan of Jack Ryan fame interrupts an attempt to kidnap the Prince of Wales and a radicalized splinter cell of the IRA wows revenge.

Michelle is a strong advocate of late Clancy.

HRBP

You have to get the compensation right.

One of the hardest things to do is refresh a board.

Almost a board within a board.

Being comfortable with having those calls.

We can't keep talking about activist wins without recognizing the great work being done by these boards.

Get the binder.

More of a convergence.

You have to sunset it.

At least sunset it.

Qatar Airways Meal Optionality

One can't say enough about the meal optionality on Qatar Airways. Vegan, with a Hindu vegan subset, Jain, Halal, etc. And all of these options might be prepared in open-space hangar-type facilities by refugees in Qatar on fixed-term contracts whose passports have been confiscated for "safekeeping."

Or so I imagine in this former limestone quarry turned park, Buttes-Chaumont, and there isn't a plane in the sky, it seems, and jogging is prevalent, with ample sweaty individual free bodies moving up and down the trails that split the greens of the park.

Qatar's vast slave-state airport is staffed by exploited refugees.

On the tarmac in Qatar at night the desert air was freezing, as cold as this park is.

Corgi!

A corgi with a slanting J-shaped tail smiles her blood-smile.

Clotilde has ripped the throat out of a wet, marbled puppy.

This corgi runs. This corgi runs on blood.

And the blood-soaked corgi in the Parc des Buttes-Chaumont isn't finished.

After the dog urinates at length on the green insectoid lamppost, its humans, who did not know that this could happen, or was possible, or feasible, watch from behind the carriage as Clotilde directs her attention to their infant, Roger.

Roger was born at 10h31 on a Friday at the Hôpital Saint-Louis. The sky was that gray marble of a November in Paris.

It is like a sink of blood has been tipped over and into the crib and the blood breaks like a wave over the sides and top of the carriage.

Winter Pre-dawn Under Museum Lights

To gain entry to the Leonardo da Vinci show, I woke up at 4h30 and avoided very ambulatory drunks and met my friend, and the friend would look at work for ages and you could almost see threads of informational content pouring into the friend that morning and in the show I ran into another person I knew who was plowing through deep comprehensive disappointment in their present unfortunate circumstance (marriage to the person next to them) and obviously there was nothing that I could do about this person's disappointment (not at that moment), nothing at all (in subsequent moments and in life), and so I returned to the subject of a perfectionist who rarely finished paintings and a gallery full of sketches and felt irritated that someone would never finish things in the pursuit of perfection, which sounded like advertising or marketing copy, and I got very attracted to one portrait in the show executed by another artist, a portrait with no logic, or insane logic, and the portrait was of a child who looked middle-aged, with a flap under his chin, and what seemed like the shadow of a beard with a bird perched somewhere on him, really just a revolting portrait that was easily the most interesting thing in the show about the hopeless perfectionist, and then I remembered Reinaldo Arenas' funny and disgusting and amazing short story about the Mona Lisa, which remained where it would forever be, in another part of the museum, not the part of the museum this show was in, and I thought of a museum open and staffed and crowded with people from everywhere, visitors and residents of the city, and transmissions and vectors and the museum employees who went on strike as the health crisis-situation materialized, and I thought about when it might possibly be that I could be stood in front of by an irritating and alive stranger while looking at a painting again.

Angers
(a Description of the Tapestries in the Hometown
of the Proprietress of a Now-defunct Bean Store
on rue Notre-Dame de Nazareth)

*

The Great Water Whore astride
The multiheaded intoxicated Lion-beast
The Great Water Whore brandishing a
Great Water Whore-sized scepter-chalice
Reduced-size Jesus in hot pink robes
Bearded and wooly haired, scared
Jesus is tiny and supported and held by
A robed angel with blue wings
The lion-beast's lion-beast balls protrude
From behind thickly muscled flanks
A lapis lazuli crown crowns
The smallest of its seven heads

*

Thick limb-thick limp bands
Solid nonliquid blood streams
From static openings
Marinating a corpse
Lapis wings lapis textile
Gripped and squished with a text
Creeping voyeur confined to voyeur nook

*

Hooded and unhooded villagers cluster
Miming fear with their hands and
Bodies but visibly unafraid facially (if this makes sense)
Clustering against a multifaceted green mound
Representing earth, the villagers watch
Demons crash into a beige city
Their webbed hands stretched out toward the sky
Tongues long and Hungarian
Horns strangely unpointed
One demon pulls down a façade as it falls
An angel explains to the sheltered voyeur
That demons are being cast out
The sheltered voyeur, essentially expressionless,
Makes an enigmatic breast-cupping gesture
So common to sheltered voyeurs
Against a blue background with violet flowers
The angel wings are pink
The roof of the voyeur shelter also is pink

*

"The tapestries are amazing—you had the chance to see them every day," I said.

"Oh, yes," the bean store salesperson replied, sadly.

There was always a kind of indomitable melancholy to this bean store proprietress, who had moved to Paris from Angers.

Why Time Passes Quickly

Victoria asked me on the pont des Arts why time passes quickly and I told her:

"Time passes quickly because as the sun rose behind the lightbox cloud cover over the canal the streetlights went off.

"Two cormorants landed in the water east of the bridge over rue de Lancry and in a short time there were more than 20 cormorants swimming, diving, hunting and stretching.

"The lock was partially open and green foamy filthy water poured through brown wooden gates as children walked masked through darkness to the opening period of 10 hours of school.

"The canal gates closed.

"The cormorants dispersed and took flight, necks rigid, bodies black and powerful against the sky.

"This is why time moves quickly, to answer your question, or why time passes *so* quickly, Victoria.

"Perceptions of things, red cat pins gifted awkwardly.

"Cormorants are part of why time passes quickly.

"The canals cormorants hunt in are full of garbage.

"Hunting cormorants in garbage water set time's pace.

"But this is not the chief determinant of time's pace.

"Marianne, the seemingly inanimate bronze incarnation of French ideals, determines the speed of perceived 'time' here for French passport holders and for those with other passports and for the stateless in France.

"Marianne's movement is so impossibly fast she appears fixed, like a hummingbird, a colibrí, which in some cultures is a warrior animal, as refugees sleep under her on the Place de la République.

"Marianne is why time moves so quickly."

"I have to go now," Victoria said.

The State of Things

Parisian businessperson with vague gestures toward a
social conscience eroded by malaise, self-indulgence and
self-regard, splashed occasionally by a fountain's whispering, sneezed upon by bébés in tiered strollers, hiding
under a conference hat from the cancer-causing sun,
riding the beige, wary of the crows, the planning crows,
attackers, when the mood strikes them, of pigeons…

The Worship of Georges Perec

An Attempt at Exhausting a Place in Paris homes in on the essential rhythms and visual vocabulary of Paris.

The fractal repetition of all forms—from the placement of spigots in a fountain to the droplets emerging from the spigots to the iron sky to the ever-repeating dances of sexually desirous pigeons, the beige buildings, the beige figurative sculptures, uniform trees buzzed unnaturally into rectangles, passionless regimented flowerbeds, beige, aristocratic immunocompromised purebreds in, for example, the Jardin du Palais Royal, close to where César Vallejo lived for a period (and thoughts of him and his cough, the death-cough of Vallejo, are on my mind)—emphasizes pounding sameness, unchanging stasis and a sort of exhaustion, an unvarying taupe drumbeat of limbo-paralysis.

Prince wrote and sang, "Holding someone is truly believing there's joy in repetition."

Georges Perec, the title of your work, executed over a period of a month of sitting in the square in front of Saint-Sulpice, might refer to this idea. The work might mean that visual content is *fixed* in Paris, but there is always some variation on what previously happened, so you get variance in repetition, as in one's exercise routine—say, running up and down the stairs every day on the canal—it varies, invariably, with different birds, different discarded bottles, different indigent wanderers, different lawyers jogging, different weather, and the same Abbas Bahktiari, actor-artist and Iranian-Persian cultural center operator, smoking cigarettes every 45 minutes, dressed impeccably.

Perec's books are apparently often "melancholy." What did Perec think of repetition and what did he think of repetition and rulemaking serving his work before dying of lung cancer in his 40s? The tantalizing thing is that Bahktiari *knows* what Perec thought of repetition —Bahktiari is Perec's translator from the French to the Farsi, and had sole access to papers that, according to Perec's will, are locked away for another 150 years, meaning that we who are alive at the time of this writing who are not Bahktiari will not have a sense of what Perec thought of repetition and attendant joy. Bahktiari knows and he's not saying anything. Future readers might, if Perec is remembered, if his books are still printed, and someone still wants access to his archives, and if those archives survive. One hopes for the best.

The cough of Perec was surely horrible, wet, resonant, like Vallejo's.

Georges Perec was a member of Oulipo, and devised constraint-based exercises to execute written work. Anne F. Garréta is part of this community with the genderless masterpiece, *Sphinx*, beautiful and strange even in translation to the English.

Binding *is release*, something sexual knotplay teaches us. The best place to learn about constraints in a sexual context in Paris is Le nœud piquant (The Spicy Noodle), located in the 16th arrondissement, close to Porte Maillot.

"The spicy noodle" is French slang for "anus."

Musette: A Visit Thwarted

Musette is a tortoiseshell cat whose territory is mainly an impasse in the 19th arrondissement. Musette lives with a human family who inhabit a house with a garden. Musette rolls on the cobblestones, does big leg stretches to get the dirty spot on her back leg, and surveys a universe of small things.

Musette herself is a hard lover, a sensuous creature full of excitement and spontaneity, impetuous, passionate, and intensely desirable. Musette will climb on human shoulders to get a better sense of her surroundings.

Deciding one morning to visit Musette later that day, a would-be visitor observed several omens. The phobic and superstitious would-be visitor decided that a visit to Musette was a bad idea.

These are the omens:

- The bloody wings of three pigeons, with no bodies nor heads to accompany them. That is to say six severed pigeon wings. It was as if a cyclops had plucked them out of a tree and feasted on their most succulent pigeon-parts (from a cycloptic perspective).

- In an expensive seafood restaurant, two elderly parents and their middle-aged, bearded son sat around a circular table that supported a tower of dead marine life on ice, claws slipping over the edges, eyes staring deadly and mutely nowhere, as the son described how this stage of his life was transpiring. Not everything on the tower was dead. Pried open oysters and clams were exposed and naked. In the reflection of a knife on the table, the birth of this middle-aged son was transpiring again, only he was his current age: He was bearded, covered in fluids and blood, and wearing a suit.

- A bright-red person sat under direct sunlight, roasting, with each hand submerged in a separate goblet of golden, glistening beer.

- A gray (fully gray, from hair to skin to eyes) man in a three-piece gray suit drank from a bottle of vodka with a gray label in front of a gray Protestant church. Beyond him and the walls behind him and through the parishioners in the church and beyond that, there was the gray convention center, designed by Christian de Portzamparc.

Musette, who had been forced to work as a rat catcher in the convention center after being trapped by the Feline Division of Christian de Portzamparc's studio, which trains cats from all over Paris to work in buildings the studio designs (the Granite Tower, the Le Monde headquarters), was rescued by Farah, a member of the convention center management and administrative staff in good standing, who brought Musette to her home, tucked into the impasse in the 19th.

*

If you are of the normal sort of person, or even if you are very strong, thoughts of home can predominate when you leave your country of origin. (It is the same for refugees and for bourgeois scum—it has never been written down before: People do think of and miss home.) There is the movement of the body of the Colombian in New York, the movement of the millions of bodies in New York and the millions of bodies in Paris and the billions of moving bodies elsewhere, there is the movement of the third party, there is the shattering of parental bones, the passage of time, the meaning of friendship, the crises of friendship, the ecstasy of friendship, Mike Immerman, the boredom and death of friendship, the severance of friendships—it's all! a rich tapestry depicting the apocalypse in a freezing castle in Angers, which the third party wants to leave now after just a few hours, for some reason, even though you took a train here just to see it, like, what is wrong with the third party, do the two of you have anything in common, anything at all? Unwilling again to focus on the death and the lockdown in Paris, weakened by middle age, I immersed myself in the past.

*

The Making of the Nightly News

Cold black eyes set in a lined, pinkish, pale face, the newscaster worshiped and idealized his father, an intercity bus driver, and so filled his large Virginia office (a corner without a view) with bus memorabilia.

Higher-level editorial meetings were held in this office with the main and secondary anchors of the nightly newscast and the producers of the newscast, and while discussing priorities from the Deepwater Horizon oil spill to the devastating earthquake in Haiti (it was in 2010), participants were surrounded by bus signs, traffic signals, bus schedules, metal and plastic models of buses, large and small, glassed in or not.

In that office, there was a piped-in soundtrack of bus-related sounds, hydraulic breaks, turn signals, old men humming to themselves in Arabic, and this newscaster was also known to pay a day rate to a sitter to emulate a waiting passenger at Union Station, and this sitter would be present for the editorial meeting, and the newscaster and his team and his main producer and the other producers would talk about how they would press an oil executive regarding an oil spill befouling the Gulf of Mexico in what at that point seemed like an irreversible unceasing ejaculation, how they would pry apart this fucking executive like a goddamned oyster in a 16th arrondissement seafood bar, and then a bus model would roll off the chief anchor's bus merchandise-laden shelves and this was so commonplace that the staff hardly noticed and went on to discuss coverage around the earthquake that had destroyed Port-au-Prince and paralyzed Haiti, a country the United States had interfered with from its liberation through to 1915, when Marines had invaded, and beyond, and the newscaster with the maniacal bus obsession that infected his marriage and his fatherhood and his workplace and even his novels, the newscaster had been a U.S. Marine in a long line of Marines. Some of these Marines had possibly been in Haiti. The earthquake had destroyed everything and the whole global community, particularly the United States of America, was engaging so passively with Haiti's tragedy, and those directing the most sober U.S. television broadcasts on the subject planned their coverage amid a mania of buses.

To reach the office in Shirlington, Virginia, from Silver Spring, Maryland, take the Red Line into Washington, D.C., and transfer to the Yellow Line, where you will see advertisements for predator drones, to the Pentagon, where workers facilitate global terror, and then take a bus that will deposit you a 10-minute walk from the building that houses the newsroom.

Friendship

Being whipped until blood is drawn with a thin, flexible, long branch by a known assailant in the mud of a park named after Jequié, the Brazilian sister city of Takoma Park (a nuclear-free zone), is no way to spend a birthday. Earlier in the evening, before the assault, at an art opening near 14th Street in Washington, D.C., John, now gone, deceased, expired, wished me a happy birthday with all the earnest intensity of more than three decades of hard-won sobriety. Being wounded by a drunken friend or adversary in the mud while he himself was drunk was something that John had certainly not experienced for 30-odd years. Possibly more. Possibly ever. Perhaps John died without knowing what it was to be assaulted in this way.

La campagne

Being in nature in form-fitting nature gear is important to him, or has become so.

He thinks about his investments and he takes his vitamins and he looks at maps and plans the next trip.

He moves compulsively through his corner of the world.

He searches for the perfect vista, a vista to end all vistas.

Once one Pacific Northwest vista is ingested and processed he moves onto the next vista, like some vista-python with bottomless capacity, unwilling to dwell on past meals.

He and she are pregnant in the wilderness.

This child will see vistas.

A Toyota that will fit them all is purchased. It cannot fit a large rug, but it fits them.

A window in their home is a polygon.

Glenstone

There is a painter and illustrator who is deeply engaged with the cats they owned and that died over a lifetime of fervent and devoted cat ownership.

Of course, the painter and illustrator remains the owner of a living cat—this artist doesn't live without cats—but the cats that have passed remain *in* the artist.

The cats have died of feline AIDS.

They were hit by cars.

They had kitty-strokes.

All manner of tragic cat-death.

These losses were devastating for the artist, because, as any cat person will tell you, each cat in this sequence, this long chain of cats, was unique and beautiful.

The artist was in their seventies now, partnered, and the artist would dream of these cats that had died. More accurately, the cats visited the artist quietly, quietly in the sense that they weren't expansive in their messaging (it was in fact sort of one-note, one-meow).

They told the artist, "You will also die."

But it wasn't aggressive and it wasn't sad, and the artist chronicled their visits, in a long, long pictorial episodic chronicle, paneled like a graphic novel.

In the resultant drawings, the cats were in their prime: 3 or 4 years old, untouched by disease, frisky and quiet or vocal, fastidious, delivering their calm message of the death to come, and their own immortality.

These works of cat visitation are housed in a single built-to-purpose building at Glenstone, a reservation-only compound of art for the wealthy (and largely art by the wealthy) in Potomac, Maryland.

An armed member of the curatorial staff guards them, much like *Guernica* is or was guarded by armed guards. The stakes are simply too high, the work too powerful, the thing being something like a world heritage site.

The artist's series is something like the armies of Darger, a universe.

A separate building on the Glenstone campus hosts the celebrated *Ad Man Studies*.

Ad Man Studies

Ad Man Studies by On Kawara illuminates selected rudiments of a life in the detailed, precision-oriented notetaking manner so characteristic of his practice.

This piece is a ledger of the sexual encounters of Mike Immerman, which includes partners of every gender and background and age group. Each description is minimal and the intention here seems to have been to provide arbitrary details about the partner, the experience, and the surroundings—e.g., Ohioan, community manager, Green-Wood cemetery—along with the date of the encounter, because this is Kawara, who devoted the last 12 years of his life (between 2002-2014) to this chronicle of Mike Immerman, and many years of his life to painting dates. Why he chose to focus on Mike Immerman as the end neared remains a total mystery. Kawara died on the day Mike Immerman left New York for Los Angeles, where Mike Immerman would meet his final sexual partner, the mother of his children, with whom he would happily grow old, and then die.

Armed Glenstone guards protect *Ad Man Studies*.

The Consequences
by Max Brett

© 2024 Max Brett
Ness Books, Paris.

All rights reserved. No part of this book may be reproduced or transmitted in any form or by any means without the written permission of the publisher.

Proofreading by
Dylan Angell

Graphic design by
Espace Ness (Julie Héneault)

Set in EB Garamond 08
Printed and bound in the EU
In an edition of 500

Published by
Ness Books
9 Passage Saint-Pierre Amelot
75011 Paris, France
espaceness.com/books

Distributed by
Antenne Books
73 Farringdon Road
London
EC1M 3JQ, United Kingdom
antennebooks.com

Achevé d'imprimer août 2024

ISBN: 9 782959 488702